WOULD YOU RATHER
for Kids

St. Patrick's Day Edition

200 Hilarious, Fun, and Cute
Questions for Kids, Teens,
and the Whole Family

Jake Jokester

How to Play
~The Rules~

- You need at least 2 players to play.

- Choose who will go first. The first player chooses a question for the next player (player 2) to answer.

- Player 2 chooses one answer out of the 2 options.

  You cannot answer "both" or neither."

  Optional rule: The answering player has to explain why they made the choice that they made.

- The player who answered the last question becomes the next asker. If there are more than 2 players, you can either pick any person to answer the next question or you can just ask the person next to you, going around in a circle.

Most important rule: Laugh, smile and have lots of fun!

Thanks for getting our book!

If you enjoy using it and it gives you lots of laughs and fun moments, we would appreciate your review on Amazon. Just head on over to this book's Amazon page and click "Write a customer review."

We read each and every one of them.

Would You Rather...

become a leprechaun

OR

become a Christmas elf?

have green hair

OR

green eyes?

Would You Rather...

sleep in a green bedroom

OR

sleep in an orange bedroom?

dress like a leprechaun

OR

dress like a vampire?

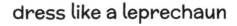

Would You Rather...

have potato-flavored candy

OR

a pickle-flavored ice cream?

speak Gaelic

OR

Latin?

Would You Rather...

get locked in a dumpster

OR

trapped in a maze?

swallow a spoon full of cinnamon

OR

a spoon full of salt?

Would You Rather...

have green cheeks when you blush

OR

get a green nose when you lie?

be a professional ice skater

OR

be an Olympic gymnast?

Would You Rather...

live in a green pea pod

OR

live in a turtle shell?

have a dog that can fit in your backpack

OR

have a dog that you can ride around on?

Would You Rather...

be bitten by a leprechaun

OR

be stung by a bee?

have a lucky four-leaf clover

OR

magic beans?

Would You Rather...

walk on a rainbow

OR

walk on stairs made of stars?

be allergic to grass

OR

be allergic to trees?

be in a sword fight

OR

be in a magical duel?

take a bite out of a stick of butter

OR

eat a spoonful of mayonnaise?

Would You Rather...

live in the mountains

OR

live on a river?

ride a bike to school

OR

ride a skateboard to school?

Would You Rather...

learn how to play the harp

OR

learn how to play the accordion?

drive a military tank

OR

drive a cruise ship?

Would You Rather...

watch a week-long movie

OR

listen to a week-long song?

eat a kale smoothie

OR

eat an asparagus jello?

Would You Rather...

have a bowl of green grapes

OR

have a bowl of sliced kiwi?

eat dirt

OR

eat grass?

Would You Rather...

steal an Olympic medal

OR

steal a piece of gold from a leprechaun?

find a gold chocolate coin

OR

find a ring pop?

Would You Rather...

get a free book

OR

get a free magazine?

play a sport you've never played before

OR

sing a song you've never heard before?

have your eyes closed in a picture

OR

accidentally make an
embarrassing face in a picture?

fight a small shark

OR

fight a giant crab?

get poked by a needle

OR

touch a burning hot plate?

have skin that sparkles in the sun

OR

hair that glows in the dark?

Would You Rather...

walk on water

OR

be able to turn water into soda?

have shoes with no soles

OR

have only one pair of underwear?

Would You Rather...

be in a dancing parade

OR

be in a traveling circus?

take a bite out of a candle

OR

a bite out of a sponge?

Would You Rather...

experience an earthquake

OR

experience a tornado?

live in a green house

OR

live in an orange house?

Would You Rather...

smell pepper spray

OR

smell fart spray?

spend the night in the woods without fire

OR

spend the night in the woods without shelter?

visit a historical park

OR

visit a famous museum?

count every star in space

OR

count every grain of sand on Earth?

Would You Rather...

win a Nobel Prize

OR

win the Eurovision Song Contest?

have 12 fingers

OR

have 8 toes?

Would You Rather...

be knighted by the Queen

OR

blessed by the Pope?

run from a volcano

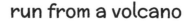

OR

run from a tsunami?

Would You Rather...

have a tail

OR

a kangaroo pouch?

live in a tree house

OR

live in a boat house?

Would You Rather...

chew on a four leaf clover

OR

chew on a plant root?

be hungry for a full day

OR

sick for a full day?

Would You Rather...

live in the White House

OR

Buckingham Palace?

wake up in medieval times

OR

wake up in Jurassic times?

have the skin of a snake

OR

the smell of a trash can?

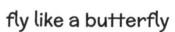

fly like a butterfly

OR

sting like a bee?

roll down a hill inside a trash can

OR

be on a swing inside the Grand Canyon?

have your breath smell like garlic

OR

have your feet smell like cheese?

be a saint

OR

be an angel?

dance like you're Irish

OR

dance like you're an Egyptian?

Would You Rather...

live inside a lighthouse

OR

live inside a submarine?

bite into a jalapeño pepper

OR

eat a stale chip?

Would You Rather...

taste a rainbow

OR

taste a cloud?

follow a rainbow

OR

follow a yellow brick road?

Would You Rather...

have a last name that is 26 letters long

OR

a first name that is only 1 letter?

have a fridge full of spinach

OR

a freezer full of peas?

Would You Rather...

have a pot of gold

OR

a pot of 100 dollar bills?

have a leprechaun for a best friend

OR

a centaur for a best friend?

Would You Rather...

eat beans for breakfast

OR

eat scrambled eggs for dessert?

visit an alternative reality

OR

visit a computer generated reality?

Would You Rather...

have hair that looks like a tennis ball

OR

hair that looks like a shaggy carpet?

have green hair

OR

green eyes?

Would You Rather...

own a jet pack

OR

own a hover board?

visit the past

OR

visit another planet?

Would You Rather...

eat soup with chopsticks

OR

eat noodles with a spoon?

eat meat from a sheep

OR

eat meat from a deer?

Would You Rather...

have chocolate-flavored lasagna

OR

lasagna-flavored chocolate?

wear a leather jacket to the beach

OR

a tank top to church?

Would You Rather...

eat pancakes made out of potatoes

OR

eat french fries made out of squash?

travel the world on a hot air balloon

OR

travel the world on a bike?

Would You Rather...

be a snake

OR

be a lizard?

eat only green foods

OR

eat only brown foods?

Would You Rather...

take a picture of a perfect rainbow

OR

take a picture of a perfect sunset?

see the world in shades of green

OR

see the world in black and white?

Would You Rather...

have a mini golf course in your backyard

OR

a tennis court in your backyard?

have half of your head shaved

OR

have the middle section
of your head shaved?

Would You Rather...

only eat vegetables

OR

only eat meat?

never have a nightmare again

OR

never have a good dream again?

Would You Rather...

squeeze lemon juice on a cut

OR

squeeze lemon juice on your eyes?

eat pickle-flavored chips

OR

avocado-flavored ice cream?

Would You Rather...

be friends with Dracula

OR

friends with a viking?

have all your hair on your back

OR

have all your hair on your arms?

Would You Rather...

see a double rainbow

OR

see the Northern lights?

bring a horse shoe to a sword fight

OR

bring a sword to a horse shoe game?

Would You Rather...

have a bright orange beard

OR

be two feet tall?

drink a root beer float

OR

drink mint chocolate shake?

Would You Rather...

be a professional golfer

OR

a professional tennis player?

find a 4-leaf clover

OR

find a needle in a haystack?

Would You Rather...

live in a flying car

OR

live underground?

bring plants back to life
with the touch of a finger

OR

create fire with the snap of a finger?

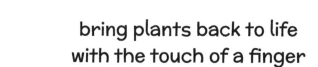

Would You Rather...

have a unibrow

OR

have long nose hairs?

be a pro wrestler

OR

an astronaut?

Would You Rather...

eat frog legs

OR

toasted crickets?

fly at the speed of a hummingbird

OR

run at the speed of a cheetah?

Would You Rather...

play a game of horse shoe

OR

a game of four square?

live in a world without internet

OR

without electricity?

Would You Rather...

have sour food

OR

spicy candy?

turn into a lobster

OR

turn into a bumble bee?

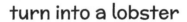

Would You Rather...

drink strong coffee

OR

bitter tea?

meet your favorite musician

OR

meet your favorite actor?

Would You Rather...

have a giant turtle as a pet

OR

a giant iguana as a pet?

spend all your money on Irish cheeses

OR

spend all your money on Irish teas?

have a glass of cucumber soda

OR

a glass of lettuce juice?

fight a leprechaun

OR

wrestle a large snake?

Would You Rather...

be related to a TV celebrity

OR

be related to a historical figure?

get pinched in the arm

OR

kicked in the leg?

Would You Rather...

eat Irish candy

OR

eat British candy?

have dinner of just green beans

OR

a dinner of just broccoli?

Would You Rather...

sleep on a pile of money

OR

sleep on a bag of gold?

make your family disappear

OR

make your friends disappear?

Would You Rather...

travel at light speed

OR

travel in reverse speed?

break a world record

OR

be the first person to walk on Mars?

Would You Rather...

have an Irish accent

OR

a Scottish accent?

never do chores again

OR

never do homework again?

Would You Rather...

have seaweed-flavored milkshake

OR

a fish-flavored cake?

own a lightsaber

OR

own Thor's hammer?

Would You Rather...

have hair that never gets wet

OR

skin that never gets sunburned?

have arms that could stretch

OR

have legs that could stretch?

Would You Rather...

have a long beard that never stops growing

OR

nails as long as your phone?

have marshmallows in your soup

OR

carrots in your cereal?

Would You Rather...

have a peanut butter celery stick

OR

a cheese stuffed bell pepper?

learn to cut your own hair

OR

learn to cook your favorite meal?

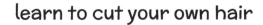

Would You Rather...

understand a foreign language

OR

discover a new language?

have a house built of stone

OR

have a house built of brick?

Would You Rather...

have green salsa

OR

red salsa?

kiss a catfish

OR

eat a sea slug?

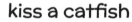

Would You Rather...

have the memory of an elephant

OR

the night vision of an owl?

have 5-foot-long arms

OR

5-foot-long legs?

Would You Rather...

have a string of bad luck
during the course of 1 day

OR

fall down a set of stairs?

be allergic to green foods

OR

allergic to the sun?

Would You Rather...

find a worm in an apple

OR

a spider in a peach?

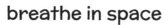

breathe in space

OR

breathe underwater?

Would You Rather...

have bad luck

OR

be born with no teeth?

have a mint-flavored popsicle

OR

a coffee-flavored toothpaste?

Would You Rather...

play in the World Cup

OR

play during an Olympic match?

fight a pigeon

OR

fight a flamingo?

Would You Rather...

have green eye lashes

OR

orange eyebrows?

eat the outside of a watermelon

OR

the outside of a banana?

Would You Rather...

disappear without saying goodbye

OR

show up to a party uninvited?

live forever

OR

make a million dollars every day?

Would You Rather...

be stuck on the edge of a cliff

OR

hang from a tall building?

always feel tired

OR

always feel hungry?

Would You Rather...

wear glasses

OR

wear braces?

eat plain cabbage

OR

plain potatoes?

have a green emerald

OR

a red ruby?

eat corned beef and cabbage

OR

ox tail soup?

Would You Rather...

have green fingernails

OR

green teeth?

live like a penguin

OR

live like a koala?

Would You Rather...

eat 1 huge grain of rice

OR

eat 100 tiny french fries?

forget how to spell the word 'luck'

OR

forget how to count to ten?

Would You Rather...

be allergic to the moon

OR

allergic to the sun?

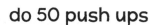

do 50 push ups

OR

run 50 yards?

Would You Rather...

eat a jar of mayonnaise

OR

eat a jar of mustard?

have a pet sheep

OR

a pet cow?

Would You Rather...

eat a bloody steak

OR

eat burnt chicken?

prank someone

OR

show someone a magic trick?

Would You Rather...

have an orange mustache

OR

a green unibrow?

wake up in ancient Ireland

OR

in ancient Greece?

Would You Rather...

be unable to stop dancing

OR

unable to stop laughing?

take a train ride across country

OR

take a boat ride to a different country?

Would You Rather...

forget how to spell

OR

have 10 years of bad luck?

have green eggs

OR

blue bacon?

Would You Rather...

never do laundry again

OR

never have to do the dishes?

eat a caramel apple

OR

a slice of apple pie?

Would You Rather...

dance in public

OR

sing in public?

upload books to your brain

OR

download memories to your computer?

Would You Rather...

be a rainbow magnet

OR

a firefly magnet?

swim in a green river

OR

take a bath in a tub full of mashed peas?

Would You Rather...

drink spoiled milk

OR

eat rotten cheese?

talk like a pirate

OR

talk like Shakespeare?

Would You Rather...

eat a clover salad with no dressing

OR

eat a dressing with no salad?

never eat salt

OR

never eat sugar?

Would You Rather...

wear horse shoes on your feet

OR

a saddle on your back?

take a bath with seaweed

OR

take a bath with tree moss?

Would You Rather...

not be able to get sunburnt

OR

not be able to get sick?

get detention at school

OR

get grounded at home?

be the size of a leprechaun

OR

have the face of an ogre?

eat a hamburger without a bun

OR

a taco without a tortilla?

Would You Rather...

bite into a raw egg

OR

get an egg throw at your face?

sleep on a bed of macaroni and cheese

OR

take a bath in maple syrup?

Would You Rather...

be as big as the sun

OR

as small as an atom?

sleep hanging upside down

OR

sleep in a coffin?

Would You Rather...

have a lucky rabbit foot

OR

a pair of lucky underwear?

move like a snake

OR

jump like a frog?

Would You Rather...

get paid to play video games

OR

get paid to watch movies?

have rain for 50 consecutive days

OR

have 50 consecutive days of no sun?

Would You Rather...

have the eyes of a cat

OR

the whiskers of a cat?

wear the coat of a sheep

OR

the fur of a wolf?

be a ghost

OR

be a zombie?

have the face of a leprechaun

OR

the face of a garden gnome?

Would You Rather...

have the power to move
rainbows with your mind

OR

move clouds with your mind?

take pictures with your eyes

OR

record noises with your ears?

Would You Rather...

lick a cactus

OR

pet an alligator?

skip school for one day

OR

go to an amusement park for one day?

Would You Rather...

have the most expensive car

OR

the most expensive house?

meet a leprechaun

OR

be a leprechaun

One last thing - we would love to hear
your feedback about this book!

If you found this activity book fun and useful, we
would be very grateful if you posted a short review on
Amazon! Your support does make a diff erence and
we read every review personally.

If you would like to leave a review, just head on
over to this book's Amazon page and click "Write a
customer review."

Thank you for your support!

Made in the USA
Las Vegas, NV
10 March 2024